pressure
cooker

pressure
cooker

Brigid Treloar

APPLE

Contents

Introducing the pressure cooker

For many busy people, time is short. There is no need, however, to rely on take-away or prepackaged meals, as enticing recipes for meat, fish, pasta, rice and even desserts can be made easily using a pressure cooker.

Cooking under pressure produces a satisfying meal in a third of the normal cooking time and also retains the flavor and nutrients of the ingredients. Meat cooked in a pressure cooker emerges fork-tender. Soups and stews develop a depth of flavor that would otherwise take an hour or more to cook.

Once you have purchased a pressure cooker, using it to prepare delicious and healthful meals is easy, efficient and economical.

Why use a pressure cooker?

- Foods cook in one-third the time because they are under pressure and therefore are cooked at a higher temperature. Cooking times for particular foods may vary depending on the pressure cooker, the heat source and the size of the food item.
- More vitamins and minerals are retained with pressure cooking than with many other cooking methods.
- The process of cooking under pressure preserves the flavor and color of foods and tenderizes foods that tend to have a tough texture.

How does a pressure cooker work?

- A pressure cooker is a pot with a locking lid. Once the pot is placed over high heat, the liquid inside comes to a boil, creating intense steam. Because the steam is trapped inside the pot, the internal temperature and pressure rise. The pressure can reach 15 pounds (7.5 kg) per square inch (PSI).
- The higher the pressure, the higher the internal temperature and the shorter the cooking time. Some pressure cookers have low and high pressure settings. Other models have a detachable pressure regulator that can adjust the pressure to low (4–5 lb/2–2.5 kg = 220°F/105°C), medium (8–10 lb/4–5 kg = 235°F/115°C) or high (15 lb/7.5 kg = 250°F/120°C).
- The lid must be locked in place for the pressure to rise inside the cooker. A safety valve automatically vents the steam.
- Using a rack or trivet to hold the food inside the pot allows it to steam above the cooking liquid rather than poach in the liquid.
- Several different foods can be placed on a rack or in a steamer basket so they cook at the same time without the flavors intermingling.

How to choose a pressure cooker

Various designs, sizes and brands of pressure cookers are available, including stove-top pots, electric pots and those designed for use in microwaves.

Traditional types have a vent with a valve that jiggles as steam is released. New designs have either a spring valve pressure regulator or a weight pressure regulator. These second-generation pressure cookers are more expensive than traditional types, but are quieter. They are also safe and versatile.

Stove-top pressure cookers

- The most common type. A good-quality stainless steel pressure cooker is an excellent long-term investment. The few rubber parts (seals) need to be replaced periodically. Aluminum and lightweight stainless steel models are less expensive but tend to develop hot spots that scorch food.
- Most pressure cookers are sold by their total liquid capacity, even though their actual usable capacity is one-half to two-thirds of the total. Common capacities are 8 quarts (8 litres), 6 quarts (6 litres) and 4 quarts (4 litres). Although 6 quarts seems to be the most popular size, buy the largest size you have room to store, especially if you want to cook large food items such as whole chicken, even if you are cooking for two.
- Choose a pot with heat-resistant handles, a locking lid that is easy to maneuver and a heavy, stainless steel base so the pot can be used for preliminary sautéing.

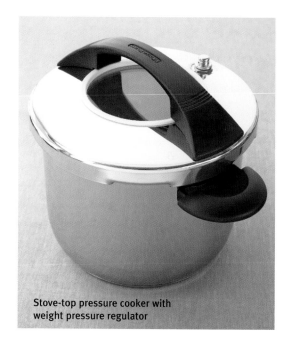

Stove-top pressure cooker with weight pressure regulator

- Look closely at the lid—the type of pressure regulator and the safety features will reveal how the cooker functions. A spring valve on the new models allows greater accuracy in timing as it is easy to see when the small colored rod, which pops up as the pressure increases, reaches high pressure.
- A quick pressure-release option avoids the need to run the cooker under cold water in order to reduce the pressure before removing the lid. This is an especially convenient feature when the pot is full and heavy or has to be brought up to pressure again for further cooking.

Spring valve pressure cooker
with two pressure settings

Stove-top pressure cooker with spring valve regulator and double handles

Stove-top pressure cooker with weight pressure regulator and bayonet handle

- Some stove-top pressure cookers have both high and low pressure settings. Others have a detachable regulator for adjusting the pressure. Most foods can be cooked at high pressure. Delicate foods such as fish and vegetables should be cooked at a lower pressure, or reduced heat, if the cooker has only one pressure setting.

Electric pressure cookers

- These cookers, though not inexpensive, are easy to operate. They have a number of preprogrammed settings for cooking selected foods.
- The disadvantage of this type is that you must wait for the electric heating elements to cool. There is no way to stop the cooking sooner. Of course, you can allow for this cooling period by subtracting it from the total cooking time.

CAUTION
ONLY PRESS THIS RELEASE IN SHORT BURSTS
UNTIL PRESSURE IS REDUCED AS HOT LIQUID
MAY BE EJECTED.

3 2 1   Steam

Remove
for cleaning

MIN   Keep
Warm
1
MAX   2
3
4
5
POWER OFF
60
50   10
40   20
30

Breville Express Cooker

Electric pressure cooker

Can I use my old pressure cooker?

- An old pressure cooker can be used if you make sure it is in good working order. Check the seals and replace them if they are worn. Examine the vent to see if it is unobstructed and will allow steam to be released. Test your cooker (see Test drive before you start, below) to see if water drips down the sides or if the pressure does not rise.
- Older models do not have the built-in safety features of the newer ones. Because they have a simple vent to release steam, they do not give a clear indication when full pressure is reached. As a result, monitoring the cooking time is even more important.
- Older models tend to use more liquid than newer spring valve models, so you will want adjust accordingly (see Test drive before you start, below). As a general rule, 1 cup (8 fl oz/250 ml) is the minimum amount required for simple vent models and ½–2 cups (4–16 fl oz/125–500 ml) for valve models. Be sure to check the owner's manual for detailed instructions.

Test drive before you start

Whether you are using an old or new pressure cooker, get to know it before you cook a recipe, so there is no chance the cooker will boil dry. Add 2 cups (16 fl oz/500 ml) water and lock the lid in place. Set the cooker over high heat and bring to full steam. Set the timer for 10 minutes. Reduce the heat just enough to maintain high pressure. This ensures that steam is still being released but not at such high force that the water inside the cooker is being depleted. After you remove the cooker from the heat and open it, measure the liquid to see how much is lost when steam is created over the 10-minute period.

Accessories

Some items come with a new pressure cooker. Others you will want to purchase and have on hand.

- A rack or trivet on which to place a heatproof plate or bowl to hold foods such as roasts above the cooking liquid.
- A steamer basket, which is often supplied with the pressure cooker, is especially useful for cooking vegetables. A bowl can be placed on the basket, or the basket can be lined with aluminum foil or parchment (baking) paper.
- A 5-cup (40–fl oz/1.25-L) heatproof soufflé dish or one that fits your pressure cooker.
- A number of ½-cup (4–fl oz/125-ml) heatproof ramekins for puddings and custards.
- A springform pan 7 or 8 inches (18 or 20 cm) in diameter for making cheesecakes.
- A heat diffuser for use under the pot to prevent rice, pasta, beans and other foods from sticking and scorching.
- A meat thermometer, especially for cuts more than 1½ inches (4 cm) thick.
- A timer, as timing is very important when using a pressure cooker.

Steamer basket

Soufflé dish

Ramekins

Springform pan

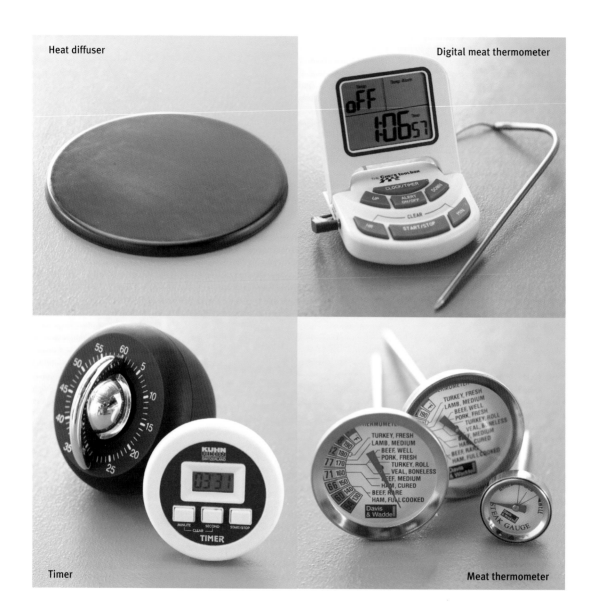

Heat diffuser

Digital meat thermometer

Timer

Meat thermometer

Aluminum foil is practical for covering ramekins and other molds and for making food parcels. It can also be used to make a holder that enables you to lower dishes or molds safely and securely into the pressure cooker.

Step 1: Begin with a 24-inch (60-cm) length of foil.

Step 2: Fold the foil lengthwise two or three times to make a long, wide strip.

Step 3: To use the strip, place the dish in the center of the strip and bring up the ends, holding one in each hand. You can now lift the dish and set it into the pressure cooker.

How should I clean and store my pressure cooker?

- Wash in hot soapy water and, if necessary, use a nonabrasive cleaner.
- Thoroughly wash the rubber seal. Rub it with vegetable oil after each use to prevent the rubber from drying out and cracking. If properly maintained, the seal should last for about 150 uses.
- Completely detach the lid from the pressure cooker and store it upside down in the cooker. This takes less room and protects the lid. Storing the cooker with the lid in place can trap odors.

Can ingredients be added during cooking?

- In some cases, they should be, especially for ingredients that require different cooking times, such as vegetables added to meat dishes. Begin with the food that needs to cook the longest. At the appropriate time, use the quick-release method (see Tips, opposite) to reduce the pressure. Remove the lid and add foods that cook for a shorter time. Replace the lid, return to pressure over high heat, then reduce the heat to maintain the pressure for the required cooking time. Adding delicate ingredients such as vegetables later prevents them from losing their inherent texture.

LEFT: When removing items after the pressure has been reduced, a cloth should be used to protect hands from the heat.

Can regular recipes be converted to the pressure cooker?

As pressure cookers reduce cooking time by about a third, simply convert by dividing the normal cooking time by three. For example, a recipe that normally takes 30 minutes would now take 10 minutes.

Pressure cooker tips

- Never fill a pressure cooker more than two-thirds full. Most cookers are marked with a line indicating the maximum level.
- Never force the lid open, as the pressure inside the cooker may not be reduced sufficiently. When removing the lid after the pressure has been reduced, always tilt it away from you to avoid being scalded by any residual steam.
- Start timing a recipe when the desired pressure is reached. Immediately reduce the heat to a level that will maintain that pressure setting, and set a timer so you know when a recipe is done.
- Use the quick-release method when adding extra ingredients to food that is already cooking or when cooking fish, vegetables or fruits. This method stops the cooking process immediately by reducing the pressure rapidly so the lid can be opened. If the pressure cooker does not have a quick-release feature, put the cooker in the sink and run cold water over the pot—but not over the vent—until the pressure drops. The pot will take longer to reheat with this method.

- When cooking different ingredients together, cut or chop them into pieces based on the cooking time required. Vegetables that need to cook longer should be cut into smaller pieces than vegetables that cook faster, thereby ensuring that all the ingredients will be done at the same time.
- Wrapping food, such as fish and vegetables, in aluminum foil or parchment (baking) paper parcels allows different seasonings to be added to different parcels, but all parcels can be cooked together.

- The flavor of fresh and dried herbs, ground spices and fresh garlic are diluted when cooked under high pressure. Therefore, increase the amount of seasonings, or add the seasonings after the pressure is released.
- Thick sauces should not be considered as cooking liquids when using a pressure cooker. Stock or water will also be required.
- Tomatoes and other ingredients with a high sugar content should be added last and not stirred in, as they tend to scorch under high pressure.
- Dairy products may be used in a pressure cooker, but it is best to add them partway into the cooking time. If added at the start, they tend to scorch. Keep in mind that at high temperatures, milk solids separate.
- Pressure cookers can be used to both defrost foods and cook them. The timing is adjusted according to the type and thickness of the food. Because the temperature in a pressure cooker is high, it is not as practical to use the cooker to thaw foods without cooking them at the same time.
- Cooking times need to be adjusted when using a pressure cooker at high altitude. Increase the time about 5 percent for every 1,000 feet (300 meters) above 2,000 feet (600 meters).

LEFT: Banana leaves can be used to make attractive parcels. See page 63 for instructions.

Trouble shooting

- If foods burn, check that the cooker has sufficient liquid or use a heat diffuser under the cooker. You can also bring the ingredients to a boil before locking the lid or bring up the pressure over a lower heat level. Another solution is to raise the food above the bottom of the pot by placing it on a trivet or steamer basket, in a heatproof bowl or in aluminum foil or parchment (baking) paper parcels.
- If water drips down the sides of the pressure cooker, the seal is probably not tight. Check the condition of the seal and replace if necessary.
- If liquid comes out of the vent, the cooker is possibly overfilled. Check the vent and make sure it is clean and free of obstructions.
- If foam comes out of the vent, especially if cooking pulses, add 1 tablespoon oil to the ingredients. Clean the vent with a pin to check no residue is caught which might block the vent.

Stocks and soups

Tips

- Always release the pressure slowly when cooking soups and stocks, or use the quick-release method of running cold water over the pressure cooker (but not the vent).
- Soups may be thickened with pureed vegetables, added at the start or during cooking, or by stirring in flour, cornstarch (cornflour), cream, sour cream, plain yogurt or bread crumbs after cooking. Add the thickener and heat the soup without boiling until it thickens. Lentils, such as split green peas, red or yellow lentils, or sweet potato, kumera, butternut and squash (pumpkin) partially dissolve as they pressure cook, thickening the stock while adding extra color and flavor.
- Substitute or add whole fish or whole chicken breasts or thighs, when making stock. Remove meat from bones and add to stock for a quick and easy soup.
- Add less liquid if adapting a conventional recipe, as less evaporation occurs when using a pressure cooker.
- Stock can be refrigerated in an airtight container for 2–3 days or frozen for 3 months if freezer operates at 65°F (-18°C).
- Always remove the scum that rises to the surface of the stock, as it tends to make the stock go cloudy.

- Chicken and vegetable stocks are usually the mildest in flavor. Because they are so easy to prepare, they are often the most useful as the basis of soups, sauces and general cooking.
- Vegetable and fish stocks should not be overcooked as their flavor can deteriorate and a bitter taste can develop. If the flavor is not strong enough after straining the solid ingredients, boil the stock briskly to reduce the water content and concentrate the flavor.
- Do not press the ingredients when straining stock as it makes the stock cloudy.
- Always start with cold water.
- For added flavor, brown vegetables and meat in olive oil or oil and butter before pressure cooking.
- If time permits, refrigerate stock so the fat rises to the surface and sets, making it easy to remove. If freezing stock, leave the fat layer on until ready to use as the fat excludes the air, which maintains the stock quality.

COOKING GUIDE FOR STOCKS

- Beef—60 minutes
- Veal—45 minutes
- Lamb—35 minutes
- Chicken—30 minutes

BASIC STOCK

MAKES ABOUT 6 CUPS (48 FL OZ/1.5 L)

3 lb (1.5 kg) chicken bones, lamb, veal or meaty beef
6 cups (48 fl oz/1.5 L) water
1 large yellow (brown) onion, peel intact, quartered
1 carrot, halved crosswise, ends removed
1 celery rib, halved crosswise
2 bay leaves
6 parsley stems
4 peppercorns

Combine all ingredients in pressure cooker. Add more water if necessary to cover ingredients. Bring to a boil over high heat. Lock lid in place and bring to high pressure over high heat. Reduce heat to a level that just maintains high pressure and cook for 30 minutes if using chicken bones, 35 minutes if using lamb, 45 minutes if using veal and 60 minutes if using beef. Remove from heat and allow pressure to reduce naturally or quick-release pressure. When stock has cooled, strain and discard solids. Skim fat from surface or, if time permits, chill stock to allow fat to congeal, then remove. Stock can be simmered further for a more concentrated flavor. Store in an airtight container in refrigerator for 3–4 days or freeze for up to 3 months.

SERVING SUGGESTION

QUICK AND EASY LENTIL SOUP WITH PANCETTA

SERVES 4

7 cups (56 fl oz/1.75 L) stock
2½ cups (1 lb/500 g) dried red lentils, rinsed
1 can (14 oz/440 g) chopped tomatoes
salt and pepper to taste

Combine ingredients in pressure cooker. Lock lid in place and bring to high pressure over high heat. Reduce heat to a level that just maintains high pressure and cook for 5 minutes. Quick-release pressure. Stir in 1–2 tablespoons balsamic vinegar and serve soup garnished with 2 oz (60 g) pancetta, prosciutto or bacon, chopped and sautéed until crisp, and chopped fresh basil or thyme.

Tip Add fresh vegetables, cooked rice or noodles, or cooked meat, chicken or seafood.

FISH STOCK

1½ lb (750 g) fish bones and heads from white-fleshed
   fish
3 or 4 lemon slices
2 yellow (brown) onions, peels intact, quartered
1 carrot, peeled and halved crosswise
2 bay leaves
6 parsley stems
4 peppercorns
8 cups (64 fl oz/2 L) water
½ cup dry white wine (optional)

Combine all ingredients in pressure cooker.
Add more water if necessary to cover
ingredients. Lock lid in place and bring to
high pressure over high heat. Reduce heat to a
level that just maintains high pressure and
cook for 5 minutes. Remove from heat and
quick-release pressure. Skim any scum from
surface to prevent stock from becoming
cloudy. When stock has cooled, strain and
discard solids. Store an airtight container in
refrigerator for 2–3 days or freeze for up to
3 months.

SERVING SUGGESTION
SEAFOOD SOUP

SERVES 4

Heat fish stock and add a selection of
uncooked seafood, such as shrimp (prawns)
and firm-fleshed white fish, cut into bite-sized
pieces. Simmer until seafood just turns white,
2–3 minutes. Add a squeeze of lemon or lime
juice and garnish with fresh chives, flat-leaf
(Italian) parsley or cilantro (coriander). For a
more substantial soup, add fresh hokkein
noodles or cooked rice.

TOMATO EGGPLANT SOUP WITH BASIL AND PARMESAN WAFERS

SERVES 4

FOR SOUP

12 large tomatoes or 2 cans (28 oz/875 g each) peeled
    whole tomatoes, crushed
2 tablespoons olive oil
2 small eggplants (aubergines), 5 oz (150 g) each,
    peels intact, finely diced
1 clove garlic, crushed
1 large yellow (brown) onion, chopped
1 cup (8 fl oz/250 ml) dry red wine
1½ cups (12 fl oz/375 ml) vegetable or chicken stock
⅓ cup (½ oz/15 g) coarsely chopped fresh basil
salt and cracked pepper

FOR PARMESAN WAFERS

1 cup (4 oz/125 g) grated Parmesan cheese

If using fresh tomatoes, put in a saucepan of boiling water and cook for 1 minute. Drain and peel, then discard skins. Coarsely chop flesh. Heat 1 tablespoon oil in pressure cooker over medium heat. Add eggplants and cook until golden, 3–4 minutes. Remove from cooker and set aside. Add remaining oil and cook garlic and onion until soft, 2–3 minutes. Add tomatoes, wine, stock and half of basil, season with salt and pepper. Lock lid in place and bring to high pressure over high heat. Reduce heat to a level that just maintains high pressure and cook for 10 minutes.

Meanwhile, make Parmesan wafers: Preheat oven to 400°F (200°C/gas mark 6). Line a baking sheet with parchment (baking) paper. Place tablespoons of Parmesan on prepared sheet, thinly spreading the cheese and leaving ½ inch (12 mm) between each tablespoonful. Cook until cheese is melted and golden, about 5 minutes. Let wafers cool on sheet. (The wafers can be made ahead and stored in an airtight container for 1 week.)

Remove cooker from heat and quick-release pressure. Add remaining basil to soup. Serve with Parmesan wafers.

SPICED SWEET POTATO, SQUASH AND SHRIMP SOUP

SERVES 4–6

2 tablespoons olive oil

8 jumbo shrimp (king prawns), peeled and deveined, tails intact

1 large yellow (brown) onion, chopped

1½ lb (750 g) sweet potatoes (kumaras), peeled and cut into 2-inch (5-cm) pieces

1 winter squash such as butternut, about 1 lb (500 g), peeled and cut into 2-inch (5-cm) pieces

4 cups (32 fl oz/1 L) chicken stock

¼ cup (2 fl oz/60 ml) tomato paste

salt and cracked pepper

2 cups (10 oz/300 g) fresh or frozen peas

1 teaspoon each ground cinnamon and ground cumin

½ cup (4 oz/125 g) thick plain yogurt or sour cream

2 tablespoons torn fresh flat-leaf (Italian) parsley

Heat 1 tablespoon oil in pressure cooker over medium heat. Add shrimp and cook, stirring occasionally, until they turn pink, 2–3 minutes. Remove from cooker and set aside. Add remaining oil and onion and cook, stirring frequently, until onion softens slightly, 2–3 minutes. Add sweet potatoes, squash, stock and tomato paste, and season with salt and pepper. Lock lid in place and bring to high pressure over high heat. Reduce heat to a level that just maintains high pressure and cook for 4 minutes. Remove cooker from heat and quick-release pressure. Working in batches, puree soup in a blender. Return soup to cooker, bring to a simmer and cook if thicker consistency is desired. Stir in peas, cinnamon and cumin and heat until peas are just cooked. Stir in yogurt. Ladle into bowls, dividing shrimp evenly. Garnish with parsley.

Tips Make mini meatballs (page 34) and cook with soup. For a vegetarian soup, omit shrimp and add other vegetables or cooked rice or barley to cooked soup.

HAM AND GREEN PEA SOUP

SERVES 4–6

FOR SOUP

1 tablespoon olive oil or unsalted butter
1 large yellow (brown) onion, diced
2½ cups (1 lb/500 g) split green peas, rinsed
2 celery ribs, coarsely chopped
7 cups (56 fl oz/1.75 L) chicken stock or water
1 ham steak or hock, about 2 lb (1 kg)
3 bay leaves
2 cloves garlic
½ teaspoon salt
2 cups (10 oz/300 g) fresh or frozen peas
¼ cup (2 oz/60 g) thick plain yogurt (optional)
2 tablespoons chopped fresh mint

SESAME TOASTS

2 pita breads, 9 inches (23 cm) in diameter, cut into triangles
1 egg white, lightly beaten
2 tablespoons sesame seeds

Heat oil in pressure cooker over medium heat. Add onion and cook, stirring frequently, until onion softens slightly, 2–3 minutes. Add split peas, celery, stock, ham, bay leaves, garlic and salt. Lock lid in place and bring to high pressure over medium heat. Reduce heat to a level that just maintains high pressure and cook for 10 minutes. Be careful that temperature is not too high or use a heat diffuser to reduce risk of peas scorching. Remove cooker from heat and allow pressure to reduce naturally for 10–15 minutes.

Meanwhile, make sesame toasts: Preheat oven to 350°F (180°C/gas mark 4). Line a baking sheet with parchment (baking) paper. Brush one side of each bread triangle with egg white and sprinkle with sesame seeds. Arrange on prepared sheet and bake until golden and crisp, 10–15 minutes.

Remove meat from any bones and stir into soup. Discard bones. Remove bay leaves and discard. Bring soup to a simmer and cook if thicker consistency is desired. Stir in peas and heat until just cooked. Ladle into bowls and garnish with yogurt and mint. Serve with sesame toasts.

SHRIMP BISQUE

SERVES 4

1 lb/500 g (about 20 medium) green shrimps (prawns),
    shells and heads on
2 tablespoons unsalted butter
1 onion, peeled and chopped
2 tablespoons plain flour
1 teaspoon sweet paprika
5 cups (40 fl oz/1.25 L) chicken or fish stock or water
1 cup (8 fl oz/250 ml) dry white wine
2 large (about 8 oz/250 g each) tomatoes or
    1 can (14 oz/440 g) chopped tomatoes
2 tablespoons tomato paste
2 bay leaves
½ cup (4fl oz/125ml) cream
¼ teaspoon salt
¼ teaspoon freshly ground white pepper
2 tablespoons cognac or brandy
1 tablespoon chopped fresh tarragon

Peel shrimp, reserving shells and heads. Cut along the top of prawns and remove the digestive tract. Heat 1 tablespoon butter in pressure cooker over medium heat. Add shrimp and cook until they turn pink, 3–4 minutes. Remove from cooker and puree, reserving 4 for garnish. Add remaining butter and onion and cook, stirring occasionally, until onion softens, 3–4 minutes. Add shrimp heads and shells and cook, stirring occasionally, until they turn red, about 5 minutes. Sprinkle flour and paprika over shrimp and cook for 2–3 minutes, stirring occasionally. Add stock, wine, tomatoes, tomato paste and bay leaves and stir to release any residue from base of cooker. Lock lid in place and bring to high pressure over high heat. Reduce heat to a level that just maintains high pressure and cook for 10 minutes. Remove cooker from heat and quick-release pressure. Remove bay leaf and puree mixture. Push mixture through a fine sieve to extract as much liquid as possible. Discard the solids. Return soup to cooker and add pureed shrimp. Stir in cream, salt, pepper and heat, but do not allow to boil. Stir in brandy. Ladle into bowls. Serve garnished with reserved prawns and tarragon.

Tips Line a colander with muslin to create a fine sieve. 1 lb (500g) shrimp shells and heads can be used instead of whole shrimps. Shrimps can be replaced with crabs and pressure cooked for about 5 minutes, depending on the size. Remove meat and follow recipe above, cooking shells for 15–20 minutes.

Meat

Tips

- Fat increases flavor, juiciness and tenderness so leave a little surface fat on the meat.
- Allow time to remove fat from the cooking liquid or sauce. If time permits, refrigerate the dish until the fat congeals and can easily be removed.
- If possible, allow the pressure to reduce naturally at the end of cooking, especially for beef. Using the quick-release method can cause meat fibers to become tough, stringy and dry. Although the meat relaxes after a resting period, it will never be as tender as when the pressure comes down naturally.
- Roasts can be difficult to brown in a pressure cooker. Therefore, meat can be browned in a small amount of oil in the pressure cooker before cooking, or it can be placed in the broiler (grill) after cooking. Large cuts of meat can be lightly brushed with soy sauce, which does not brown the meat but adds color and enhances flavor without dominating the other seasonings.
- Meat can be lightly coated with flour before browning in the pressure cooker. Be sure to stir any residual flour into the stock or other cooking liquid so it does not stick to the bottom of the cooker.

- After browning the meat, scrape any browned bits of food from the bottom of the cooker, to add flavor to the dish and to prevent food from scorching as it cooks.
- After the meat is done, the cooking liquid can be boiled to reduce and thicken it, or it can be thickened with cornstarch (cornflour) or flour. For each 1 cup (8 fl oz/250 ml) of liquid, use 1 tablespoon flour or cornstarch mixed with enough water to make a smooth paste. Egg yolk, cream, sour cream, plain yogurt or pureed vegetables may also be used as a thickener. Add the thickener and heat, without boiling, until sauce reaches desired consistency.

Cooking frozen meat

- Cook 5 minutes longer under high pressure for each inch (2.5 cm) of thickness.
- Allow an extra 10 minutes per pound (500 g) when pot-roasting a frozen bone-in cut of meat.
- To reheat frozen cooked meat casseroles, place the frozen food in the pressure cooker with ⅔ cup (150 ml) water or stock. Lock the lid in place and bring to high pressure. Reduce the heat and cook for 5–10 minutes, depending on thickness of meat.

Pot-roasting

- Large bone-in cuts of meat must have sufficient room for the steam to circulate or they may not cook evenly.
- Meat should not exceed 3 pounds (1.5 kg) for a 6-quart (6-L) pressure cooker.
- Use a trivet inside the cooker and place the meat on the trivet. Stock or water is added to the cooker, and the meat cooks above the liquid.

Stewing and braising

- Cooking times will depend on the size and thickness of the pieces of meat, not weight.
- Liquid can be reduced to 1¾ cups (14 fl oz/440 ml) for stewing but never below 1¼ cups (10 fl oz/300 ml) because of the long cooking times.

Meat thermometer temperatures

Beef, lamb and veal

Rare	120°–130°F (49°-54°C)
Medium rare	130°–135°F (54°–57°C)
Medium	140°–150°F (60°–65°C)
Medium well	155°–165°F (68°–74°C)
Well done	170°–185°F (77°–85°C)

Pork

Medium	155°–165°F (68°–74°C)
Well done	180°–185°F (82°–85°C)

Chicken and turkey

Well done	160°F (71°C)
White meat (breast)	160°F (71°C)
Dark meat (legs)	170°F (77°C)

MEAT COOKING GUIDE

Cooking times may vary slightly, depending on the quantity of meat and the size of the cooker.

Beef roasts—High pressure, natural release

- Round (top side), sirloin (rump) —20–25 minutes per lb (500 g)
- Chuck (more than 2 inches/5 cm thick) —15 minutes per lb (500 g)
- Corned (salt) beef, brisket —15 minutes per lb (500 g)
- Chuck steak
- Cubes (1–1½ inches/2–2.5cm) —20–25 minutes
- Oxtails—30 minutes
- Ground (minced) beef—10 minutes

Lamb roasts

- Shoulder (boned and rolled) —17 minutes per lb (500 g)
- Leg, loin—17 minutes per lb/500g
- Chops—10 minutes

Pork roasts

- Loin—15 minutes per lb (500 g)
- Shoulder (boned and rolled) —15 minutes per lb (500 g)
- Chops, fillets, cutlets—10 minutes

Veal

- Neck, loin, boned shoulder —12 minutes per lb (500 g)
- Chops and cutlets—10 minutes

BEEF CURRY WITH RICE

SERVES 4

This recipe cooks the rice and curry together in 6- or 8-quart (6- or 8-L) pressure cooker. For smaller cookers, rice may have to be cooked separately.

1 cup (8 fl oz/250 ml) water
1/3 cup (3 oz/90 g) Indian curry paste, or to taste
1 1/2 lb (750 g) boneless beef round (topside), cut into
    strips 2 inches (5 cm) long and 1/2 inch (12 mm) wide
1 yellow (brown) onion, diced
1 1/2 cups (10 1/2 oz/315 g) long-grain white rice, rinsed
3 cups (24 fl oz/750 ml) water or beef stock
1/2 teaspoon salt (optional)
2 tablespoons cornstarch (cornflour)
1 cup (8 oz/250 g) plain yogurt
1/2 cup (3 oz/90 g) raisins
1/2 cup (2 oz/60 g) coarsely chopped unsalted
    cashews, toasted

Combine water and curry paste in pressure cooker. Add beef and onion. Place trivet in cooker. Put rice, water and salt (if using) in an aluminum foil–lined steamer basket or heatproof bowl and use a foil strip (page 15) to lower onto trivet. Lock lid in place and bring to high pressure over high heat. Reduce heat to a level that just maintains high pressure and cook for 4 minutes. Remove cooker from heat and allow pressure to reduce naturally for 8 minutes, then quick-release. Remove rice, cover and keep warm. Remove trivet. Mix cornstarch with enough water to make a thin paste. Stir into curry and cook over medium heat until sauce thickens, 2–3 minutes. Stir in yogurt and raisins. Serve with rice and garnish with cashews.

Tip For Thai curry, omit raisins and cashews. Use Thai red curry paste and substitute coconut milk for yogurt. Garnish with chopped fresh cilantro (coriander), bean sprouts, sliced green onion, thinly sliced red chili, and lime wedges.

MEATBALLS WITH BASIL-TOMATO SAUCE AND SPAGHETTI

SERVES 4

FOR MEATBALLS

1½ lb (750 g) ground (minced) beef

2 large eggs, lightly beaten

1 yellow (brown) onion, finely diced

1 celery rib, finely diced

1 clove garlic, crushed

2 teaspoons mixed dried herbs such as marjoram,
    thyme and rosemary

1 cup (4 oz/125 g) dried bread crumbs

2 tablespoons tomato paste

2 tablespoons Worcestershire sauce

2 tablespoons olive oil

FOR SAUCE AND SPAGHETTI

3 cups (24 fl oz/750 ml) chicken or beef stock

¾ lb (375 g) spaghetti or egg noodles

1 teaspoon salt

2 tablespoons olive oil

1 can (14 oz/440 g) whole tomatoes with juice

1 teaspoon mixed dried herbs such as thyme, oregano
    and marjoram

½ cup (2 oz/60 g) chopped, drained oil-packed sun-
    dried tomatoes or 1½ cups (9 oz/280 g) cherry
    tomatoes, halved

2 tablespoons Worcestershire sauce

¼ cup (2 fl oz/60 ml) dry red wine (optional)

⅓ cup (½ oz/15 g) chopped fresh basil

½ cup (2 oz/60 g) grated Parmesan cheese

To make meatballs, in a bowl mix together beef, eggs, onion, celery, garlic, herbs, bread crumbs, tomato paste and Worcestershire sauce. Using dampened hands, shape mixture into 12 balls. Heat 1 tablespoon oil in pressure cooker over medium-high heat. Add meatballs in 2 or 3 batches and cook, turning occasionally, until brown, 3–4 minutes, adding extra oil if needed. Using a slotted spoon, remove meatballs from cooker, being careful not to break them, and set aside.

To make sauce and spaghetti, bring stock to boil in pressure cooker. Stir in noodles, salt and oil and stir well. Place meatballs on noodles and pour canned or fresh tomatoes on top, but do not stir. Lock lid in place and bring to high pressure over high heat. Reduce heat to a level that just maintains high pressure and cook for 5 minutes. Remove cooker from heat and quick-release pressure. Stir gently to separate noodles and release any stuck to bottom of cooker. Stir in herbs, sun-dried tomatoes, red wine (if using) and basil and cook over medium heat until heated through. Serve garnished with Parmesan cheese.

ITALIAN HERB AND RED WINE POT ROAST

SERVES 4

HERB MIX
4 cloves garlic
⅓ cup chopped fresh parsley leaves
8 large fresh sage leaves
¼ cup chopped fresh sage leaves

3 tablespoons olive oil
3lb (1.5kg) beef pot roast (rump, chuck, topside),
    excess fat removed
¾lb (12oz) button or Swiss brown mushrooms, wiped
    and thinly sliced
1 onion, peeled and coarsely chopped
1 carrot, peeled and coarsely chopped
1 celery stick with leaves, coarsely chopped
2 bay leaves, lightly crushed
2 tablespoons tomato paste
1 cup (8fl oz/250ml) dry red wine
1 cup (8fl oz/250ml) beef or chicken stock
1 teaspoon salt
cracked black pepper
4 large (about 7oz/220g each) new potatoes, washed
1–2 tablespoons cornstarch (cornflour), mixed with
    2–3 tablespoons cold water (optional)

Mince herbs in food processor. Set aside half and combine the other half with 1½ tablespoons oil. Make about 12 deep slits in the roast and, using a teaspoon and fingers, stuff the slits with the herb mix. Heat remaining oil in the pressure cooker over a moderate heat. Add the roast and brown evenly on all sides, about 15 minutes. Remove roast and cook mushrooms over high heat, stirring occasionally, until browned, about 4 minutes. Remove and cook onion, carrot, celery and bay leaves until onion lightly browned, about 4 minutes. Add remaining herb mix, tomato paste and ½ cup red wine and cook until reduced by half. Stir in remaining wine, stock, salt and pepper.

Place roast in the broth with potatoes around the roast. Lock lid in place and bring to high pressure over high heat. Reduce heat to a level that just maintains high pressure and cook for 40 minutes. Remove cooker from heat and allow pressure to reduce naturally. Remove potatoes and roast, cover with foil and rest for 10 minutes before carving. Strain broth, remove bay leaves and excess fat. Puree vegetables, return to cooker with broth and mushrooms and heat. If a thicker gravy is required, stir in cornstarch and heat until thickened, about 2 minutes.

Tips
• Potatoes can be served whole or mashed with a little cream or butter.
• Slice meat and return to cooker to reheat and absorb some of the gravy.

BEER AND MUSTARD CORNED BEEF

SERVES 4

3 lb (1.5 kg) corned (salt) beef
2 large yellow (brown) onions, thickly sliced
2 large carrots, peeled and thickly sliced
2 celery stalks, coarsely chopped
4 bay leaves
1 lemon, thickly sliced
salt and cracked pepper
¾ cup (6 fl oz/185 ml) water
3 tablespoons whole-grain Dijon mustard, or to taste
1½ cups (12 fl oz/375 ml) beer
2–3 tablespoons cornstarch (cornflour)

Remove most of fat from meat, leaving a little for flavor. Put onions, carrots, celery, bay leaves and lemon in pressure cooker. Season with salt and pepper. Combine water and mustard and pour over vegetables. Put meat in pot and pour beer over top, but do not stir. Lock lid in place and bring to high pressure over high heat. Reduce heat to a level that just maintains high pressure and cook for 55 minutes. Remove cooker from heat and allow pressure to reduce naturally, about 15 minutes.

Remove beef and keep warm. Strain cooking liquid and skim fat from surface. Remove bay leaves and lemon slices from vegetables. Transfer vegetables to a food processor and puree. Return pureed vegetables and liquid to pot. If desired, simmer liquid to reduce and add extra mustard. Mix cornstarch with enough water to make a thin paste. Stir into liquid and cook over medium heat, stirring occasionally, until thickened, 2–3 minutes. To serve, slice beef and top with sauce.

Tip The corned beef can be accompanied by potatoes and cabbage. Quick-release pressure after cooking beef for 25 minutes. Add 2 lbs (1 kg) unpeeled potatoes to pressure cooker. Return to high pressure and cook for remaining 30 minutes. Peel potatoes and dice. Toss with ⅓ cup (½ oz/15 g) chopped fresh flat-leaf (Italian) parsley and 1 tablespoon unsalted butter. If desired, cut 1 savoy cabbage into wedges, leaving stem intact, and cook in pressure cooker for 3 minutes, then quick-release pressure.

OSSO BUCCO AND GARLIC WHITE BEANS

SERVES 4

2–3 tablespoons olive oil

3 lb (1.5 kg) veal shanks, cut into slices 1–1½ inches
   (2.5–4 cm) thick

1 large yellow (brown) onion, diced

1 carrot, peeled and diced

4 cups (32 fl oz/1 L) veal or chicken stock

1 cup (8 fl oz/250 ml) dry white wine

1 tablespoon balsamic vinegar

2 cloves garlic

2 bay leaves

1 teaspoon salt

cracked pepper

2 cups (14 oz/440 g) dried cannellini beans, rinsed

1 large tomato, about ¼ lb (125 g), diced

FOR GREMOLATA

1 cup (1½ oz/45 g) tightly packed, chopped, fresh
   flat-leaf (Italian) parsley leaves

1–2 teaspoon finely grated lemon zest

1 clove garlic, crushed

Heat 1 tablespoon oil in pressure cooker over medium heat. Working in batches, add veal and brown on each side, 2–3 minutes, adding more oil if needed. Remove and set aside. Add remaining oil and cook onion and carrot, stirring occasionally, until vegetables soften slightly, 1–2 minutes. Add stock, wine, vinegar, garlic, bay leaves, salt, pepper to taste, beans and tomato. Lock lid in place and bring to high pressure over high heat. Reduce heat to a level that just maintains high pressure and cook for 10 minutes. Remove cooker from heat and quick-release pressure. Add veal to cooker. Lock lid in place and return cooker to high pressure over high heat. Reduce heat to a level that just maintains high pressure and cook for 20 minutes.

Meanwhile, make gremolata: Place all ingredients in a bowl and stir thoroughly to combine. Set aside.

Remove cooker from heat and allow pressure to reduce naturally, about 15 minutes. Strain and remove and discard bay leaves. If desired, simmer cooking liquid for 5–10 minutes to thicken. Arrange veal, beans and vegetables on plates, top with sauce (if using) and garnish with gremolata.

PORK WITH PORT, CHERRIES AND SAGE

SERVES 4

1–2 tablespoons olive oil
3 lb (1.5 kg) boneless pork shoulder, trimmed of fat
1 red onion, diced
1 cup (5 oz/150 g) fresh or canned cherries, pitted
1 cup (8 fl oz/250 ml) port
1 cup (8 fl oz/250 ml) chicken stock
2 tablespoons balsamic vinegar
24 fresh sage leaves
½ teaspoon salt
Mashed Parsnips and Celery Root (page 68)

Heat 1 tablespoon oil in pressure cooker over medium heat. Add pork and brown on all sides, 2–3 minutes per side. Remove and set aside. Add onion and cook until slightly softened, about 2 minutes, adding more oil if necessary. Add pork, cherries, port, stock, vinegar, 20 sage leaves and salt. Lock lid in place and bring to high pressure over high heat. Reduce heat to a level that just maintains high pressure and cook for 35 minutes. Remove cooker from heat and allow pressure to reduce naturally for about 10 minutes, then quick-release pressure. Remove pork and keep warm. Skim fat from cooking liquid, transfer liquid to a saucepan and keep warm. If desired, simmer cooking liquid for 5–10 minutes to thicken. Slice meat and serve topped with sauce and garnished with a sage leaf. Accompany with Mashed Parsnips and Celery Root.

Tips If using canned cherries, add juice to cooking liquid. Marinate pork in port for 1–2 hours, if time permits.

Poultry

Tips

- The pressure cooker should be large enough to allow sufficient space around a whole chicken so that steam will circulate and promote even cooking. If the cooker is not large enough, cut the chicken into portions.
- Chicken can be difficult to brown in a pressure cooker. Therefore, it can be browned in a small amount of oil in the pressure cooker before cooking, or it can be placed in the broiler (grill) after cooking. Alternatively, chicken can be lightly brushed with soy sauce, which does not brown the chicken but adds color and enhances flavor.
- Although quick release of steam after cooking does not toughen chicken as it does beef, a better texture is achieved if the pressure is released slowly. This also makes the skin less likely to split.
- As a guide, allow the steam to reduce naturally for 4 minutes after cooking, then quick-release by putting the cooker in the sink and running cold water over the cooker (but not the vent). Alternatively, reduce the cooking time by 1–2 minutes and allow the pressure to reduce naturally for about 10–15 minutes, before removing the lid.
- Cooking times are the same for one piece or multiple pieces, but an extra 5–10 minutes may be required if the pressure cooker is full. Check doneness after the minimum cooking time and return to pressure to cook longer if needed.

POULTRY COOKING GUIDE

Times may vary slightly with the quantity of chicken and size of the pressure cooker used.

Chicken

- Whole chicken—6 minutes per lb (500 g); 8 minutes with stuffing
- Chicken quarters or mixed parts—8 minutes
- Chicken breast halves, boneless—4 minutes
- Chicken breast halves, bone in—7 minutes
- Chicken thighs, boneless—4 minutes
- Chicken thighs, bone in—8 minutes
- Chicken drumsticks—8 minutes
- Whole legs—8 minutes
- Chicken and turkey, cubed (1 inch/2.5 cm)—4 minutes

Duck

- Duck, mixed pieces—15–18 minutes, depending on size

Turkey

- Turkey, mixed pieces—12–15 minutes, depending on size
- Turkey breast half—10 minutes per lb (500 g)

CHICKEN CHETTINAD

SERVES 4–6

2 lb (1 kg) skinless, boneless chicken thighs, cut into
    1-inch (2.5-cm) pieces
½ cup (4 fl oz/125 ml) buttermilk or ½ cup
    (4 oz/126 g) plain yogurt
⅓ cup (3 oz/90 g) unsalted butter
⅓ cup (3 fl oz/90 ml) canola oil
1 cinnamon stick
3 green cardamom pods, cracked
3 whole cloves
1 teaspoon asafetida
5 yellow (brown) onions, chopped
2½ tablespoons peeled and finely grated fresh ginger
6 cloves garlic, crushed
1 tablespoons chili powder
2½ tablespoons ground coriander
4 teaspoons ground turmeric
salt
½ cup (4 fl oz/125 ml) water
8 tomatoes, chopped, or 1 can (14 oz/440 g) chopped
    tomatoes
1 cup (1½ oz/45g) chopped fresh cilantro (coriander)
1 tablespoon crushed peppercorns
12 fresh curry leaves
steamed basmati rice (see White Rice page 75)

In a nonreactive bowl, combine chicken and
buttermilk. Cover and marinate in refrigerator
until needed. Melt butter with oil in pressure
cooker over medium heat. Add cinnamon,
cardamom and cloves and cook until fragrant,
about 30 seconds. Stir in asafoetida, then
onions. Cook until onions are dark and
golden, 10–15 minutes. Add ginger, garlic, chili
powder, coriander and turmeric and season
with salt. Stir until fragrant, about 1 minute.
Add chicken and buttermilk marinade, then
water. Pour tomatoes over top but do not stir.
Lock lid in place and bring to high pressure
over high heat. Reduce heat to a level that just
maintains high pressure and cook for 4
minutes. Remove cooker from heat and quick-
release pressure. If desired, simmer over low
heat to thicken sauce, 5–10 minutes. Stir in
cilantro, peppercorns and curry leaves. Serve
with basmati rice.

Tip This recipe is very hot. Halve the
quantities of chili and peppercorns if a milder
dish is desired.

CHICKEN WITH BELL PEPPER, POTATOES AND OLIVES

SERVES 4

1–2 tablespoons olive oil

2 lb (1 kg) boneless, skinless chicken thighs

¾ cup (6 fl oz/180 ml) chicken stock or water

¾ cup (6 fl oz/180 ml) red wine vinegar

1 large yellow (brown) onion, diced

1 can (13 oz/400 g) tomatoes with juice

1¼ lb (625 g) new potatoes

½ small red bell pepper (capsicum), about 2 oz (60 g), seeded and cut into thin strips

1 cup (4 oz/125 g) kalamata olives, pitted

2 tablespoons capers, rinsed and drained (optional)

⅓ cup (½ oz/15 g) chopped fresh flat-leaf (Italian) parsley

Heat oil in pressure cooker. Working in batches, cook chicken, stirring occasionally, until browned, 4–5 minutes. Remove chicken and set aside. Wipe cooker with paper towels. Return chicken to cooker with stock, vinegar and onion. Pour tomatoes over top but do not stir. Scatter potatoes on top. Lock lid in place and bring to high pressure over high heat. Reduce heat to a level that just maintains high pressure and cook for 4 minutes. Remove cooker from heat and allow pressure to reduce naturally for about 4 minutes, then quick-release pressure. If desired, simmer over low heat to thicken sauce, 5–10 minutes. Stir in olives and capers (if using). Garnish with parsley.

EGGPLANT, POTATO AND CHICKEN PIE

SERVES 6

1 lb (500 g) ground (minced) chicken

1 celery rib, finely diced

1/4 cup (1 oz/30 g) rolled oats

1 large egg, lightly beaten

1 tablespoon teriyaki sauce

2 tablespoons sweet chili sauce

1 teaspoon peeled and grated fresh ginger
  or 1/4 teaspoon ground ginger

3 tablespoons olive oil

1 eggplant (aubergine), 3/4 lb (375 g), peel intact, cut
  into slices 1/4 inch (6 mm) thick

1 yellow (brown) onion, sliced

2 large potatoes such as Desiree or Yukon gold, about
  3/4 lb (375 g) each, peeled and cut into slices
  1/4 inch (6 mm) thick

2 sweet potatoes (kumeras), about 3/4 lb (375 g),
  peeled and cut into slices 1/4 inch (6 mm) thick

2 cups (16 fl oz/500 ml) chicken stock

1/2 cup (4 oz/125 g) sour cream

Combine chicken, celery, oats, egg, teriyaki and chili sauces and ginger in a bowl and mix well. Heat 1 tablespoon oil in pressure cooker over medium heat. Working in batches, cook eggplant slices, turning once, until lightly browned, 3–4 minutes total. Remove and set aside. Add remaining oil and cook onion until softened slightly, 2–3 minutes. Arrange half of potato and sweet potato slices and onions in bottom of steamer basket. Cover with half of eggplant slices and then chicken mixture. Cover with remaining eggplant slices and onion and then remaining potato and sweet potato slices. Set trivet in pressure cooker. Place basket on trivet and pour in stock.

Lock lid in place and bring to high pressure over high heat. Reduce heat to a level that just maintains high pressure and cook for 14 minutes. Remove cooker from heat and allow pressure to reduce naturally for 4 minutes, then quick-release pressure. Meanwhile, preheat broiler (grill). Remove basket from cooker. Set a plate over basket and invert. Carefully remove basket. Spread sour cream over top of pie and broil (grill) until golden, about 5 minutes. Cut pie into wedges.

Tip Serve pie accompanied by a mixed green salad.

WHOLE CHICKEN WITH FIG, PECAN AND ROSEMARY STUFFING

SERVES 4

1 cup (2 oz/60 g) fresh bread crumbs

⅓ cup (2 oz/60 g) chopped dried figs and 8 dried figs, halved

4 scallions (shallots/spring onions), finely sliced

⅓ cup (2 oz/60 g) chopped pecans

2 tablespoons chopped fresh rosemary leaves

2 tablespoons balsamic vinegar

4 lb (2 kg) whole chicken, rinsed and dried with paper towel

1 tablespoon olive oil

3 cups (24 fl oz/750 ml) chicken or vegetable stock

2 garlic cloves, finely chopped

2 tablespoons cornstarch (cornflour)

½ cup (4 fl oz/125 ml) marsala, wine or sherry

salt and cracked black pepper

Combine bread crumbs, ⅓ cup figs, onion, pecans, rosemary and 1 tablespoon balsamic vinegar. Stuff mixture in chicken cavity, sealing the opening with toothpicks.

Heat pressure cooker on moderately hot and add oil. Rub chicken with remaining balsamic vinegar and cook breast side down, until golden, about 2-3 minutes. Carefully turn with 2 wooden spoons or tongs to brown the underside. Remove the cooker from heat, put chicken on a plate and discard oil.

Put trivet in the cooker and add stock, garlic and figs. Put chicken in the basket on the trivet, breast side up. Lock lid and bring to high pressure over high heat. Reduce heat to a level that just maintains high pressure and cook for 25 minutes. Remove from heat and allow pressure to reduce naturally for 10-15 minutes. Remove chicken, cover with foil.

Remove fat from stock. Combine cornflour and marsala and stir into stock. Season to taste and heat until sauce thickens. Serve chicken with sauce.

LEMON-HERB CHICKEN WITH MASHED POTATOES AND SPINACH

SERVES 4

1–2 tablespoons olive oil

2 leeks or small yellow (brown) onions, sliced

3 lb (1.5 kg) skinless, bone-in chicken thighs and half breasts

3 cloves garlic

¼ cup (⅓ oz/ 10 g) fresh rosemary leaves plus 4 sprigs for garnish

2 tablespoons fresh thyme leaves

1 cup (8 fl oz/250 ml) chicken stock

½ cup (4 fl oz/125 ml) dry white wine

2 tablespoons soy sauce

finely grated zest and juice of 2 lemons

1¼ lb (625 g) baking potatoes, peeled and quartered

1–2 tablespoons unsalted butter

¼–⅓ cup (2–3 fl oz/60–90 ml) milk or light sour cream

salt and cracked pepper

2 cups (4 oz/125 g) shredded spinach, rinsed and dried

Heat 1 tablespoon oil in pressure cooker over medium heat. Add leeks and cook, stirring occasionally, until softened, 3–4 minutes. Remove and set aside. Working in batches, add chicken and cook, turning as needed, until browned, 3–4 minutes, adding more oil if needed. Add leeks, garlic, herbs, stock, wine, soy sauce and lemon zest and juice. Scatter potatoes over chicken. Lock lid in place and bring to high pressure over high heat. Reduce heat to a level that just maintains high pressure

and cook for 8 minutes. Remove cooker from heat and allow pressure to reduce naturally, 7–10 minutes. Remove potatoes and chicken from cooker and set aside. Simmer liquid over low heat if a thicker sauce is desired. Put chicken and sauce in a serving dish and keep warm. Return potatoes to cooker and mash with a potato masher. Stir in butter and milk and season to taste with salt and pepper. Stir in spinach.

DUCK AND GREEN CHILI CURRY

SERVES 4

FOR SPICE PASTE

2 green Thai or Anaheim chili peppers, seeded and
    coarsely chopped
1 yellow (brown) onion, coarsely chopped
2 teaspoons ground turmeric
1 tablespoon ground coriander
1 tablespoon coarsely chopped raw cashews
2 teaspoons peeled and grated fresh ginger
4 cloves garlic, coarsely chopped
2 peppercorns
2 tablespoons water
3 tablespoons canola oil
2 bay leaves
1 lemongrass stalk, white part only, bruised
1/2 teaspoon dried shrimp paste

1 lb (500 g) skin-on, boneless duck or chicken breasts,
    cut into 1-inch (2.5-cm) cubes
1 cup (8 fl oz/250 ml) water
16 fresh basil leaves
1 tablespoon tamarind paste or lemon juice
steamed basmati rice (see White Rice page 75)

To make spice paste, combine all ingredients in a food processor and process until a thick paste forms.

Heat 2 tablespoons oil in pressure cooker over medium heat. Add spice paste and cook until fragrant, about 1 minute. Add bay leaves, lemongrass and shrimp paste and cook for 1 minute. Add duck and cook, stirring frequently, until golden, 4–5 minutes. Pour in water. Lock lid in place and bring to high pressure over high heat. Reduce heat to a level that just maintains high pressure and cook for 4 minutes. Remove cooker from heat and allow pressure to reduce naturally for 4 minutes, then quick-release pressure.

Meanwhile, heat remaining oil in small frying pan over medium heat. Working in batches, fry basil leaves until crisp, turning as needed. Transfer to paper towels to drain. Remove bay leaves and lemongrass from cooker and discard. Stir in tamarind paste. Garnish with fried basil. Serve with basmati rice.

CHICKEN BREASTS STUFFED WITH FETA CHEESE AND SPINACH

SERVES 4

About ¾ cup (5 oz/150 g) spinach, chopped, drained,
   cooked
2 oz (60 g) feta cheese or goat cheese, crumbled
2 teaspoons pine nuts, toasted
1 tablespoon fresh lemon thyme or 1 teaspoon finely
   grated lemon zest
1 clove garlic, crushed
salt and cracked pepper
4 skinless, boneless chicken half breasts,
   7–8 oz (220–225 g) each, tenderloins removed
2–3 tablespoons olive oil
1¼ lb (20 oz/625 g) new potatoes, cut into quarters
2 leeks, thinly sliced crosswise
½ cup (4 fl oz/125 ml) chicken stock
½ cup (4 fl oz/125 ml) dry white wine

In a bowl, stir together spinach, cheese, pine nuts, thyme and garlic, and season with salt and pepper. Make a slit in one long side of each chicken breast to create a pocket. Fill pocket with spinach mixture and close securely with toothpicks. Heat 1 tablespoon oil in pressure cooker over medium heat. Add stuffed breasts and cook until lightly browned on each side, 2–3 minutes. Remove and set aside. Add potatoes and cook, stirring occasionally, until browned all over, about 5 minutes, adding more oil if needed. Remove and set aside. Add leeks and sauté until softened slightly, 2–3 minutes. Set trivet in cooker and pour in stock and wine.

Put chicken in steamer basket or heat-proof bowl. Lower onto trivet with foil strips (see page 15). Scatter potatoes on top. Lock lid in place and bring to high pressure over high heat. Reduce heat to a level that just maintains high pressure and cook for 8 minutes. Remove cooker from heat and allow pressure to reduce naturally for 4 minutes, then quick-release pressure. Remove steamer basket and transfer chicken and potatoes to a serving dish and keep warm. Remove trivet. Simmer leeks and cooking liquid if thicker sauce is desired. Pour sauce over chicken.

Tip Marinate chicken in equal quantities of lemon juice and olive oil for 1–2 hours.

Fish and seafood

Tips

- Although fish cooks quickly with other stove-top methods, using a pressure cooker keeps it moist.
- Cooking time is determined by the thickness of the fish, not by weight.
- Fish can be placed in a steamer basket or on a rack or plate on the trivet. It can also be enclosed in a parcel made of aluminum foil, parchment (baking) paper or blanched banana leaves (page 63). Add extra time for cooking parcels, especially foil.
- Fish can be steamed in a steamer basket above rice or potatoes cooking in the liquid below.
- Another benefit of parcels is that they can be flavored individually to suit the different tastes of diners. One easy option is to squeeze lemon or lime juice or drizzle white wine over the fish, then season with salt and pepper before wrapping.
- Fish can be cooked on a sheet of parchment (baking) paper for easy removal from the pressure cooker and to facilitate cleanup.
- Cooking juices can be frozen and used to make fish stock.
- Frozen fish fillets and shellfish can be cooked in the pressure cooker without defrosting or adjusting cooking times. Twice as much liquid will accumulate in the cooker at the end of cooking, because as the fish thaws, it releases both water and juices.
- Fish is cooked when the flesh turns white or opaque and when the flesh flakes easily when tested with a fork.
- As it is easy to overcook seafood, always use the quick-release method of reducing pressure by running cold water over the pressure cooker (but not the vent).

FISH COOKING GUIDE

- 1 inch (2.5 cm) thick—5 minutes
- 1 inch (2.5 cm) thick in parchment (baking) paper—7–8 minutes
- 1 inch (2.5 cm) thick in aluminum foil—12–13 minutes

OCTOPUS IN HERBED RED WINE

SERVES 4

2 lb (1 kg) cleaned baby octopus, cut into bite-sized pieces

1 yellow (brown) onion, diced

1 serrano or other red chili pepper, seeded and finely chopped (optional)

⅔ cup (5 fl oz/150 ml) dry red wine

¼ cup (2 fl oz/60 ml) red wine vinegar

¼ cup (⅓ oz/10 g) fresh basil, chopped

2 cloves garlic

2 bay leaves

1 teaspoon salt

1 can (14 oz/440 g) whole tomatoes with juice

1 teaspoon lemon zest, finely grated

¼ cup (⅓ oz/10 g) fresh flat-leaf (Italian) parsley, chopped

Combine octopus, onion, chili, wine, vinegar, basil, garlic, bay leaves and salt in pressure cooker. Pour tomatoes over top but do not stir in. Lock lid in place and bring to high pressure over high heat. Reduce heat to a level that just maintains high pressure and cook for 10 minutes. Remove cooker from heat and allow pressure to reduce naturally for about 10 minutes. If desired, simmer over low heat to thicken sauce, 5–10 minutes. Remove and discard bay leaves. Stir in lemon zest and parsley. Serve with white wine risotto or green salad.

CRAB SPINACH SOUFFLÉ WITH WALNUT CRUST

SERVES 4

1 tablespoon butter, at room temperature

60 g walnuts, toasted and finely chopped, or bread
crumbs

1 lb/500 g cooked crab meat, tuna or salmon, chopped

½ cup (4 oz/125 g) English spinach, blanched,
drained, or baby rocket

2 ½ cups (5 oz/150 g) fresh white bread crumbs

2 oz/60 g grated Parmesan or Swiss cheese

2 scallions (shallots/spring onions), finely chopped

1 teaspoon grated lemon rind

1 cup (4 fl oz/250 ml) warm milk

5 eggs, separated

¼ teaspoon salt

cracked black pepper

3 cups (24 fl oz/750 ml) water

Generously butter 6-cup (48 fl oz/1.5 litre) ovenproof soufflé dish. Sprinkle the insides with walnuts. Combine crab, spinach, bread crumbs, cheese, scallions, lemon and milk. Stir in egg yolks, salt and pepper. Whisk egg whites until stiff. Gently fold into fish mix with a metal spoon. Pour into soufflé dish, cover with lightly greased, pleated foil to allow soufflé to rise and tie with string. Put dish in basket. Place trivet in cooker and add water. Put basket on trivet, lock lid in place and bring to high pressure on high heat. Reduce heat to a level that just maintains high pressure and cook for 15 minutes. Remove from heat quick-release pressure. Soufflé is cooked when skewer inserted in middle comes out clean. Serve immediately.

Tip Although the top will sink, the soufflé can also be served cold with a salad.

FISH FILLETS IN COCONUT SAUCE

SERVES 4

2–3 tablespoons peanut or corn oil

1 teaspoon brown or black mustard seeds

½ teaspoon fenugreek seeds

2 teaspoons dried red chili flakes or red pepper flakes

3 yellow (brown) onions, about 1 lb (500 g) total, halved and thinly sliced

2 tablespoons fresh ginger, peeled and grated

4 cloves garlic, crushed

36 fresh curry leaves

3 teaspoons ground turmeric

2 tomatoes, about ½ lb (250 g) total, coarsely chopped

1½ cups (12 fl oz/375 ml) coconut cream

salt

1 lb (500 g) firm, white-fleshed fish fillets such as ocean perch, lingcod, blue eye or barramundi, skin removed and flesh cut into 2-inch (5-cm) pieces

juice of 1 lemon

steamed basmati rice (see White Rice page 75)

Heat oil in pressure cooker over low heat. Add mustard seeds and cook, stirring, until seeds crackle, about 30 seconds. Add fenugreek seeds and red pepper flakes and cook, stirring, until seeds turn light golden brown and pepper flakes are deep golden brown, about 30 seconds. Add onions, ginger and garlic, and cook, stirring, for 1 minute. Add curry leaves and turmeric and cook, stirring, for 30 seconds. Add tomatoes and cook until slightly soft, about 3 minutes. Stir in coconut cream

and season with salt. Stir in fish pieces. Lock lid in place and bring to high pressure over high heat. Remove cooker from heat and quick-release pressure. Stir in lemon juice. Serve with steamed rice.

Tip Curry sauce can be transferred to a bowl before cooking fish. Rice can be cooked in bottom of pressure cooker by placing bowl holding fish on a trivet above rice. Cooking time is longer if fish is cooked in a bowl. Halve the quantity of chili flakes or red pepper flakes if a milder dish is desired.

MEDITERRANEAN FISH PARCELS WITH COUSCOUS

SERVES 4

2 large oranges

1 tablespoon lemon juice

1½ teaspoons ground allspice

¼ teaspoon ground cumin

¼ teaspoon ground ginger

½ teaspoon salt

cracked pepper

1 clove garlic, crushed

1 fennel bulb, trimmed and thinly sliced crosswise

1 tablespoon Pernod

4 firm, white-fleshed fish fillets such as ocean perch, lingcod, blue eye or swordfish, about 6 oz (180 g) each

½ lb (250 g) instant couscous

1 cup (8 fl oz/250 ml) boiling water

½ cup (4 oz/125 g) unsalted butter, melted

½ cup (3 oz/90 g) golden raisins (sultanas)

⅓ cup (½ oz/15 g) each chopped fresh flat-leaf (Italian) parsley and fresh cilantro (coriander)

Cut 1 orange into slices. Remove zest from remaining orange, then juice. In a bowl, stir together orange juice and zest, lemon juice, spices and salt, and season with pepper. Add fennel and Pernod. In a bowl, combine couscous and boiling water, then stir in butter, raisins, parsley and cilantro. Divide couscous among four 12-inch (30-cm) squares of parchment (baking) paper or aluminum foil. Arrange a fillet on couscous, then top with fennel mixture and orange slices, dividing

evenly. Bring up opposite edges of each square and fold over, then twist ends to seal. Add 1 cup (8 fl oz/250 ml) water to pressure cooker. Place a trivet in cooker. Arrange fish in steamer basket and place on trivet. Lock lid in place and bring to high pressure over high heat. Reduce heat to a level that just maintains high pressure and cook for 7–8 minutes if using parchment, 12–13 minutes if using foil (times may vary, depending on thickness of fish). Remove cooker from heat and quick-release pressure. Remove parcels and serve.

Tip Banana leaves may be used to make parcels. Trim rough edges and cut each leaf into a 12-inch (30-cm) square. Dip in boiling water for about 30 seconds to soften. Plunge leaves into cold water to set color. Following recipe above, arrange couscous, fish, fennel mixture and orange slices at one end of each leaf. Carefully fold over, tucking in sides, to create a parcel. Secure with toothpicks or kitchen string. Cook parcels for 8 minutes.

Vegetables

Tips

- Vegetables can be cooked in liquid in the pressure cooker or steamed above the liquid. Steaming is ideal for delicate vegetables.
- Pressure cooking is particularly well suited to root vegetables. Do not cook sweet potatoes (kumaras) whole as they burst before being cooked through.
- Many vegetables cook so quickly in the pressure cooker that they easily lose their shape and texture, making them appropriate for mashing.
- To reduce the likelihood of skins splitting, reduce the cooking time by 3 minutes and let the pressure release naturally.
- Removing the skins from vegetables such as potatoes is easier after cooking than when the food is raw.
- In general, always use the quick-release method for lowering the pressure to prevent vegetables from overcooking.
- As for cooking fish, vegetables may be enclosed in aluminum foil or parchment (baking) paper parcels and cooked above the liquid, allowing extra time, especially for foil parcels.
- Vegetables with different cooking times can be cooked together. Start with those that need the longest time and add others according to the time they require.

Alternatively, cut vegetables that need longer cooking into smaller pieces than those that cook faster, as for the Mashed Parsnips and Celery Root on page 68.

VEGETABLE COOKING GUIDE

- Artichokes, whole, 6–7 oz (180–220 g) —6–8 minutes
- Beets (beetroots), whole, about 5 oz (150 g)—20–22 minutes
- Beets, slices, ¼ inch (6 mm) thick —3–5 minutes
- Carrots, slices, ¼ inch (6 mm) thick —4–5 minutes
- Celery root, chunks, 1 inch (2.5 cm) —6–7 minutes
- Parsnips, chunks, 1 inch (2.5 cm) —5–6 minutes
- Potatoes, baking, whole, about 10 oz (300 g)—30 minutes; about 5 oz (150 g) —15 minutes
- Potatoes, baking, chunks, 1 inch (2.5 cm) —6–7 minutes
- Potatoes, new, whole, 2 oz (60 g) —8–9 minutes; 1 oz (30 g)—5–6 minutes
- Sweet potatoes (kumeras), chunks, 2 inches (5 cm)—9–10 minutes
- Turnips, chunks, 2 inches (5 cm) —7–8 minutes

CREAMY MASHED POTATOES

SERVES 4

¾ lb (375 g) sweet potatoes (kumaras), peeled and
  cut into 2-inch (5-cm) pieces
¾ lb (375 g) baking potatoes, peeled cut into 2-inch
  (5-cm) pieces
1 yellow (brown) onion, diced
1 clove garlic
1–2 tablespoons unsalted butter
¼–⅓ cup (2–3 fl oz/60–90 ml) light sour cream or
  milk
salt and cracked pepper
¼ cup (⅓ oz/10 g) chopped flat-leaf (Italian) parsley,
  chopped

Pour 1 cup (8 fl oz/250 ml) water into
pressure cooker and set trivet inside. Put both
potato types, onion and garlic in steamer
basket or a flat-bottomed dish, lowered onto
trivet with foil strips (see page 15). Lock lid in
place and bring to high pressure over high
heat. Reduce heat to a level that just maintains
high pressure and cook for 10 minutes.
Remove cooker from heat and quick-release
pressure. Remove vegetables and set aside.
Remove trivet and pour liquid from cooker.
Return vegetables to cooker and mash with a
potato masher. Stir in butter and sour cream,
and season with salt and pepper. Stir in parsley.

Tip For one-pot cooking, vegetables can
be added to stews or roasts during the last
10 minutes of cooking. When they are
done, remove meat from cooker and mash
vegetables, adding sour cream, butter and
herbs, following recipe above.

HERBED POTATO AND PEAR SALAD

Any amount of potatoes may be cooked to make this quick and easy salad.

Pour 1 cup (8 fl oz/250 ml) water into pressure cooker and set trivet inside. Put bite-sized potato chunks or baby new potatoes in a steamer basket or heatproof dish. Lower onto trivet with foil strips (see page 15). Lock lid in place and bring to high pressure over high heat. Reduce heat to a level that just maintains high pressure and cook for 6 minutes if using a steamer basket and slightly longer if using a dish. Remove cooker from heat and allow pressure to reduce naturally for 5–10 minutes. Transfer potatoes to a bowl and let cool. Fold in the following: good-quality mayonnaise or plain yogurt; firm pear with skin intact, finely diced; chopped fresh flat-leaf (Italian) parsley; squeeze of lemon; wasabi or horseradish to taste.

MASHED PARSNIPS AND CELERY ROOT

SERVES 4

1 lb (500 g) parsnips, peeled and cut into 1-inch (2.5-cm) chunks
1 lb (500 g) celery root (celeriac), peeled and cut into ¾-inch (2-cm) chunks
1–2 tablespoons unsalted butter
2–3 tablespoons heavy (double) cream (optional)
salt and cracked pepper

Pour 1 cup (8 fl oz/250 ml) water into pressure cooker and set trivet inside. Put parsnips and celery root in steamer basket or heatproof bowl. Lower onto trivet with foil strips (see page 15). Lock lid in place and bring to high pressure over high heat. Reduce heat to a level that just maintains high pressure and cook for 5 minutes. Remove cooker from heat and quick-release pressure. Remove vegetables. Remove trivet and drain liquid from cooker. Return vegetables to cooker and mash with a potato masher. Stir in butter and cream, and season with salt and pepper.

BABY BEET, ORANGE AND NUT SALAD

SERVES 4

FOR SALAD

2 bunches small (about 1 ½ lb/750 g) beets
  (beetroot), washed and trimmed
2 oranges, peeled and segmented
1 red onion, thinly sliced
3 cups (3 oz/90 g) baby English spinach or rocket
⅓ cup (1 ½ oz/50 g) hazelnuts, toasted, skinned and
  coarsely chopped

FOR DRESSING

¼ cup extra virgin olive oil
¼ cup rice vinegar
1 tablespoon chopped fresh mint leaves
salt and cracked black pepper

Pour 2 cups (16 fl oz/500 ml) water in
pressure cooker and set trivet inside. Trim
stems from beets (beetroots), leaving about
1 inch (2.5 cm) attached so beets do not bleed
during cooking. Wash beets and put in steamer
basket. Lock lid in place and bring to high
pressure over high heat. Reduce heat to a level
that just maintains high pressure and cook for
about 13 minutes for small beets (4 oz/125 g
each). Remove cooker from heat and quick-
release pressure. When beets are cool enough
to handle, peel away skins and cut beets into
wedges. Place in bowl and toss with orange
slices, onion, hazelnuts and baby spinach leaves.

For dressing: Whisk all ingredients together.
Add dressing to salad as desired.

RATATOUILLE

SERVES 4

3 tablespoons olive oil

1 large (8 oz/250 g) yellow onion, peeled and cut into
about 10 wedges

4 baby (10 oz/300 g) eggplants (aubergines), cut into
1-inch (2.5-cm) pieces, skin on

2 garlic cloves, crushed

2 medium (10oz/300g) zucchini, cut into 3/4-inch
(2-cm) slices

2 medium (14oz/440g) red bell peppers, seeded and
chopped into 1-inch (2.5-cm) squares

14 oz/400 g fresh tomatoes, skinned and seeded or
canned whole tomatoes

1/4 cup (2oz/60ml) water or vegetable stock

1 tablespoon balsamic vinegar

3–4 sprigs fresh thyme

3/4 teaspoon salt

cracked black pepper

2 tablespoons chopped fresh basil or parsley

Heat oil in pressure cooker over moderately low heat. Add onion, eggplant and garlic and cook 5 minutes, stirring occasionally. Add remaining ingredients, except basil. Lock lid and bring to high pressure on high heat. Reduce heat to a level that just maintains high pressure and cook 3–5 minutes, the longer time for softer vegetables. Remove heat and quick-release pressure. Serve hot or cold, garnished with basil.

Tip Serve this dish on its own or as an accompaniment to chicken, fish or with pasta. For an easy main meal, cook fish fillets (eg. ocean trout or salmon) in steaming basket, placed directly on top of vegetables.

VEGETABLES IN THAI RED CURRY SAUCE

SERVES 4

1 tablespoon peanut or corn oil
¼ cup (2 fl oz/60 ml) Thai red curry paste
4–5 cups (1–1½ lb/500–750 g) diced, firm-textured
    vegetables (sweet potato/kumera, carrots,
    cauliflower)
1 cup (8 fl oz/250 ml) chicken or vegetable stock
coconut cream, to taste
chopped fresh cilantro (coriander) for garnish

Heat oil in pressure cooker over medium heat.
Add Thai red curry paste and cook until
fragrant, 3–4 minutes. Add diced vegetables
and stock. Lock lid in place and bring to high
pressure over high heat. Reduce heat to a level
that just maintains high pressure and cook
4 minutes, or longer if softer vegetables
preferred. Remove cooker from heat and
quick-release pressure. Stir in coconut cream
to taste and garnish with chopped fresh
cilantro (coriander). If a thicker consistency is
preferred, simmer until liquid reduces.

Tip Add cooked or canned soy beans or tofu
for a more substantial dish.

VEGETABLE BRAISE

SERVES 4

2 tablespoons olive oil
2 medium (12oz/375g) red onions, peeled and cut into
    wedges
8 oz/250 g mushrooms, quartered
2 garlic cloves, crushed
½ cup (4 fl oz/125 ml) dry white wine
3 lb/1.5kg mixed root vegetables (such as swede,
    turnips, carrot, parsnip, celeriac),
peeled and cut into 1-inch (2.5-cm) cubes
⅓ cup (2oz/60g) red lentils, rinsed
2 cups vegetable or chicken stock
1 tablespoon plain flour
½ teaspoon salt
cracked black pepper
1 tablespoon Dijon mustard (optional)
½ cup fresh parsley, chopped, or ¼ cup fresh thyme

Heat oil in pressure cooker over moderately
low heat. Add onion and cook 5 minutes,
stirring occasionally. Add mushrooms and
garlic, and cook over moderate heat for
3 minutes, stirring occasionally. Add wine
and heat until nearly all absorbed. Stir in
vegetables, lentils, stock, flour, salt and pepper.
Lock lid in place and bring to high pressure
over high heat. Reduce heat to a level
that just maintains high pressure and cook
6 minutes. Remove from heat and quick-
release pressure. Stir in mustard and parsley.

Grains, beans and pasta

Tips for cooking grains and beans

- Do not fill the pressure cooker more than half full when cooking rice, dried beans, lentils or other foods that absorb liquid and expand, as the vent can become clogged during cooking.
- Cook brown rice and other whole grains in plenty of water, as you would pasta, so there is no chance all the liquid is absorbed, thereby causing grains to scorch. A heat diffuser can be used to help prevent scorching and sticking.
- Soaking dried beans overnight will reduce the cooking time by about half.
- A variety of grains can be cooked together. If the cooking times vary greatly, start with the grain that needs to cook longer, then quick-release the pressure and add ingredients that cook for less time. Alternatively, soak the long-cooking grain overnight in water to cover, which will the reduce cooking time by about half.
- To prevent sputtering at the vent after cooking grains, quick-release the pressure by running cold water over the cooker, but not the vent.
- Always clean the pressure cooker after cooking grains in case the vent or regulator has become blocked.
- Letting the pressure reduce naturally will help prevent the skins of beans splitting.
- Add 1 tablespoon oil to beans to reduce foaming.

Tips for cooking rice

- Rice can be cooked directly in the pressure cooker liquid, in a steamer basket lined with aluminum foil or in a heatproof dish placed on the trivet. This latter option allows the rice to be served in the same dish, but takes slightly longer to cook.
- Although cooking rice in a pressure cooker does not save a great deal of time, it has the advantage of being relatively foolproof. In addition, a one-dish meal such as paella can be prepared in the cooker.
- Rice should be cooked with at least 1 tablespoon oil or butter to reduce foaming that may clog the vent.
- The timing and amount of liquid needed can vary with different pressure cookers. If the rice is not done after the recommended cooking time, do not continue to cook under pressure unless sufficient liquid is in the cooker. If no liquid remains, cover cooker rice and let rice steam, or add extra liquid and simmer on the stove top over low heat.
- When increasing the quantity of rice being cooked, the amount of water is not increased proportionally, but the cooking time remains the same.

COOKING GUIDE

Rice

LONG-GRAIN WHITE
Quantity 1 cup (7 oz/220 g)
Liquid 1½ cups (12 fl oz/375 ml)
Yield 3 cups (15 oz/470 g)
Cooking time 5 minutes + natural release

BASMATI
Quantity 1 cup (7 oz/220 g)
Liquid 1½ cups (12 fl oz/375 ml)
Yield 4½ cups (22½ oz/705 g)
Cooking time 5 minutes + natural release

Quantity 2 cups (14 oz/440 g)
Liquid 3 cups (24 fl oz/750 ml)
Yield 3 cups (15 oz/470 g)
Cooking time 5 minutes + natural release

LONG GRAIN IN A BOWL
Quantity 1 cup (7 oz/220 g)
Liquid 1½ cups (12 fl oz/375 ml)
Yield 3 cups (15 oz/470 g)
Cooking time 7 minutes + natural release

SHORT GRAIN BROWN
Quantity 1 cup (7 oz/220 g)
Liquid 4 cups (32 fl oz/1 L)
Yield 2 cups (10 oz/300 g)
Cooking time 15 minutes + quick release

Quantity 2 cups (14 oz/440 g)
Liquid 7 cups (56 fl oz/1.75 L)
Yield 4½ cups (22½ oz/705 g)
Cooking time 15 minutes + quick release

WILD RICE
Quantity 1 cup (7 oz/220 g)
Liquid 3–4 cups (24–36 fl oz/750 ml–1 L)
Yield 2¾ cups (13 oz/400 g)
Cooking time 15–20 minutes + quick release

Beans

PEARL BARLEY
Quantity 1 cup (6 oz/180 g)
Liquid 3 cups (24 fl oz/750 ml)
Yield 2½ cups (15 oz/470 g)
Cooking time 20 minutes + quick release

CANNELLINI
Quantity 1 cup (7 oz/220 g)
Liquid 3–4 cups (24–36 fl oz/750 ml–1 L)
Yield 2 cups (14 oz/440 g)
Cooking time 28–32 minutes + natural release

CHICKPEAS
Quantity 1 cup (6 oz/180 g)
Liquid 3–4 cups (24–36 fl oz/750 ml–1 L)
Yield 2½ cups (16 oz/500 g)
Cooking time 32–35 minutes + quick release

LENTILS (RED, BROWN, FRENCH)

Quantity 1 cup (7 oz/220 g)
Liquid 3–4 cups (24–36 fl oz/750 ml–1 L)
Yield 2 cups (15 oz/470 g)
Cooking time 1–5 minutes + quick release

PEAS (SPLIT, YELLOW, GREEN)

Quantity 1 cup (7 oz/220 g)
Liquid 3–4 cups (24–36 fl oz/750 ml–1 L)
Yield 2 cups (16 oz/500 g)
Cooking time 10–12 minutes + quick release

RED KIDNEY BEANS

Quantity 1 cup (7 oz/220 g)
Liquid 3–4 cups (24–36 fl oz/750 ml–1 L)
Yield 2 cups (16 oz/500 g)
Cooking time 25–30 minutes + natural release

WHITE RICE

MAKES 3 CUPS (15 OZ/470 G)

1 tablespoon olive oil or unsalted butter
1 cup (7 oz/220g) long-grain white or basmati rice,
   rinsed
1½ cups (12 fl oz/375 ml) water or chicken, beef or
   vegetable stock
½ teaspoon salt (optional)

Heat oil in pressure cooker over medium-high heat. Add rice and stir to coat with oil. Add water and salt (if using). Lock lid in place and bring to high pressure over high heat. Reduce heat to a level that just maintains high pressure and cook for 5 minutes. Remove cooker from heat and allow pressure to reduce naturally for 7–10 minutes.

Tip The oil is added to reduce foaming that may clog the vent.

WHITE RICE IN A DISH

MAKES 3 CUPS (15 OZ/470 G)

This method allows other ingredients, such as meat, to be cooked underneath at the same time.

1 cup (7 oz/220g) long-grain white rice, rinsed
1½ cups (12 fl oz/375 ml) water or chicken, beef or vegetable stock
½ teaspoon salt (optional)

Set trivet in pressure cooker and pour in 1 cup (8 fl oz/250 ml) water. Line steamer basket with aluminum foil or use a flat-bottomed, heatproof dish (such as a soufflé dish with a capacity of 5–7 cups/40–56 fl oz/1.25–1.75 L) that will sit on trivet while allowing steam to circulate in cooker. Combine rice, water and salt (if using), in lined steamer or dish. Lower onto trivet with foil strips (see page 15). Lock lid in place and bring to high pressure over high heat. Reduce heat to a level that just maintains high pressure and cook for 5 minutes. Remove cooker from heat and allow pressure to reduce naturally for 7–10 minutes. Lift out dish and serve.

Tip Cooking rice in a bowl or foil-lined steaming tray will slightly increase cooking time.

BROWN RICE

MAKES ABOUT 3 CUPS (15 OZ/470 G)

1½ cups (10½ oz/315 g) short-grain brown rice, rinsed
5½ cups (44 fl oz/1.35 L) water or chicken, beef, or vegetable stock
1 tablespoon olive oil or unsalted butter
¾ teaspoon salt (optional)

Combine rice, water, oil and salt (if using) in pressure cooker. Lock lid in place and bring to high pressure over high heat. Reduce heat to a level that just maintains high pressure and cook for 15 minutes. Remove cooker from heat and quick-release pressure.

GARLIC EGGPLANT AND SPLIT PEAS

MAKES ABOUT 2¹/₂ CUPS

3 tablespoons olive oil

1 small (12 oz/375 g) eggplant (aubergine), peeled and
    diced into 1-inch (2.5-cm) cubes

2 garlic cloves, crushed

1 cup (6oz/185g) yellow split peas

2 cups water or vegetable stock

1 teaspoon salt

cracked black pepper

1 teaspoon ground cumin

1 tablespoon lime or lemon juice

¹/₄ cup chopped sun-dried tomatoes in oil, drained
    or cherry tomatoes, diced (optional)

2 tablespoons fresh mint leaves, chopped

Heat 3 tablespoons oil in pressure cooker over moderately low heat. Add eggplant and garlic and cook for 5 minutes, stirring occasionally. Add split peas, stock, salt and pepper. Place cooker over a heat mat, if available, to prevent peas catching on base. Lock lid in place and bring to high pressure over high heat. Reduce heat to a level that just maintains high pressure and cook for 10 minutes. Remove from heat and quick-release pressure. Stir with wooden spoon to puree mixture. Add cumin, juice and tomatoes, stirring to combine. Garnish with mint.

Tips Use as a dip with vegetable sticks or toasted Lebanese bread or dilute with extra juice, stock or water and use as a sauce with fish, chicken or tofu. Add 1 cup (2 oz/60 g) blanched, finely chopped English spinach or 1 cup (8 oz/250 ml) yogurt for variation.

PAELLA

SERVES 4

2 tablespoons olive oil

1 large yellow (brown) onion, cut into thin wedges

1 clove garlic, crushed

1 chorizo, about 6 oz (180 g), sliced crosswise

2 teaspoons smoked paprika or 1 tablespoon sweet
  paprika

2 cups (14 oz/440 g) long-grain rice

1 lb (500 g) skinless, boneless chicken thighs, diced

1 cup (8 fl oz/250 ml) chicken stock

2 bay leaves

1 teaspoon salt

1 can (14 oz/440 g) whole tomatoes with juice

2 cups (8 oz/250 g) frozen green peas, defrosted

1 cup (6 oz/185 g) chopped roasted red bell peppers
  (capsicums) or 1 fresh red bell pepper, seeded and
  chopped

1 cup (5 oz/150 g) pitted black olives in brine, rinsed

1 tablespoon fresh lemon thyme leaves

2 tablespoons fresh flat-leaf (Italian) parsley, chopped

1 lemon, cut into 8 wedges

Heat 1 tablespoon oil in pressure cooker over
medium heat. Add onion, garlic and chorizo
and cook until onion is slightly softened, 3–4
minutes. Stir in paprika and rice. Add chicken,
stock, bay leaves and salt. Pour tomatoes over
chicken but do not stir in. Lock lid in place
and bring to high pressure over high heat.
Reduce heat to a level that just maintains high
pressure and cook for 3 minutes. Remove
cooker from heat and allow pressure to reduce

naturally for 6 minutes, then quick-release
pressure. Remove and discard bay leaves. Stir in
peas, bell peppers, olives and thyme and heat
through. Garnish with parsley and lemon
wedges.

RISOTTO WITH RED WINE, SPINACH AND THYME

SERVES 4

1 tablespoon olive oil or unsalted butter

2 red onions, diced

1½ cups (10½ oz/315 g) Carnaroli, Vialone Nano or
  Arborio rice

1 cup (8 fl oz/250 ml) dry red wine

3–4 cups (24–32 fl oz/750 ml–1 L) chicken stock

1 teaspoon salt

cracked pepper

2 cups (4 oz/125 g) baby spinach leaves, chopped

2 tablespoons balsamic vinegar

2 tablespoons chopped fresh thyme or flat-leaf
  (Italian) parsley

1 cup (4 oz/125 g) Parmesan cheese, grated

Heat oil in pressure cooker over medium heat. Add onions and cook, stirring occasionally, until softened slightly, 1–2 minutes. Add rice and stir to coat with oil. Add wine and stir until absorbed, 30–60 seconds. Stir in 3 cups stock and salt and season with pepper. Scrape bottom of pot to release any rice. Lock lid in place and bring to high pressure over high heat. Reduce heat to a level that just maintains high pressure and cook for 4 minutes. Remove cooker from heat and quick-release pressure. Continue to cook over medium heat, stirring, for 3–5 minutes, adding remaining stock if needed. Stir in spinach, vinegar, thyme and some of cheese, reserving remainder for garnishing at table.

Tip To make risotto a main course, panfry or steam shrimp (prawns) and/or scallops, then stir into or serve on top of risotto.

MIDDLE EASTERN BROWN RICE AND CHICKPEAS

SERVES 4

1 tablespoon olive oil or unsalted butter

1 large yellow (brown) onion, diced

2 cloves garlic, crushed

1½ teaspoons cumin seeds

1½ cups (11 oz/330g) short-grain brown rice, rinsed

½ cup (3 oz/90 g) dried chickpeas (garbanzo beans),
   rinsed and soaked overnight in water to cover

5½ cups (44 fl oz/1.35 L) chicken stock

1 teaspoon salt

1 teaspoon ground cinnamon

1 cup (4 oz/125g) mixed dried fruits such as golden
   raisins (sultanas), chopped apricots and chopped
   apples

1 winter squash such as butternut, about 10 oz (300 g),
   cut into 1-inch (2.5-cm) pieces

1 cup (5 oz/150g) slivered almonds, toasted

½ cup (¾ oz/20g) fresh cilantro (coriander) or
   flat-leaf (Italian) parsley, chopped

Heat oil in pressure cooker over medium heat. Add onion, garlic and cumin seeds and cook, stirring occasionally, until onion softens slightly, about 2 minutes. Add rice and stir to coat with oil. Add chickpeas, stock, salt, cinnamon and dried fruit. Lock lid in place and bring to high pressure over high heat. Reduce heat to a level that just maintains high pressure and cook for 15 minutes. Remove cooker from heat and quick-release pressure. Add squash, lock lid in place and bring to high pressure over high heat. Reduce heat to a level that just maintains high pressure and cook for 3 minutes. Remove cooker from heat and quick-release pressure. Stir in almonds and cilantro.

Tip To make a main dish, heat 1 tablespoon olive oil in a frying pan. Lightly brown 1 lb (500 g) boneless leg of lamb or boneless chicken thighs, cut into 1-inch (2.5-cm) cubes. After rice has cooked for 14 minutes, quick-release pressure and add lamb or chicken. Lock lid in place and bring to high pressure over high heat. Reduce heat to a level that just maintains high pressure and cook for 4 minutes. Quick-release pressure. Serve with mango chutney.

VEGETABLE LASAGNE

SERVES 4

About 5 tablespoons (3 fl oz/90 ml) olive oil

1 eggplant (aubergine), about 6 oz (180 g), skin intact, cut crosswise into slices 1/3 inch (9 mm) thick

1 butternut or other winter squash, about 9 oz (280 g), peeled, quartered lengthwise and cut into slices 1/4 inch (6 mm) thick

1 yellow (brown) onion, cut into slices 1/4 inch (6 mm) thick

1 clove garlic, crushed

2 1/2 cups (20 fl oz/625 ml) good-quality pasta sauce

1 cup (4 oz/125 g) sliced pitted black olives in brine, rinsed

1/2–1 lb (250–500 g) no-boil lasagna noodles

1 large zucchini (courgette), cut lengthwise into slices 1/4 inch (6 mm) thick

1/3 cup (1 1/2 oz/45 g) Parmesan cheese, grated

Heat 1 tablespoon oil in pressure cooker over medium heat. Add half of eggplant slices and cook until soft and golden on both sides, 3–4 minutes. Transfer to paper towels to drain. Cook remaining slices, adding 1 tablespoon oil if needed. Heat 1 tablespoon oil and cook butternut squash slices until golden on both sides, 3–4 minutes. Transfer to paper towels to drain. Heat 1 tablespoon oil and cook onion until golden, 3–4 minutes. Remove and set aside. In a bowl, combine garlic, sauce and olives.

Put 1/2 cup (4 fl oz/125 ml) sauce in bottom of a soufflé dish with a diameter of 7–8 inches (18–20 cm). Cover with a layer of lasagna noodles, breaking them to fit. Cover noodles with a thin layer of butternut squash, onion, eggplant and zucchini. Top with 1/2 cup sauce. Repeat layers, finishing with a layer of lasagna noodles and then a layer of pasta sauce. Sprinkle evenly with Parmesan cheese.

Set trivet in pressure cooker and add 3 cups (24 fl oz/750 ml) water. Lower soufflé dish onto trivet with foil strips (see page 15). Lock lid in place and bring to high pressure over high heat. Reduce heat to a level that just maintains high pressure and cook for 30 minutes. Remove cooker from heat and quick-release pressure. Insert knife into center; if lasagna is done, knife should slide in easily. If necessary, lock lid in place, return to high pressure and cook longer. Lift out dish and serve.

Desserts

LIME AND MANGO RICE

SERVES 4

Although the rice pudding can be cooked in one step, it is very easy for it to scorch and the milk to separate. Cooking it as you would a risotto avoids these problems but takes a few minutes longer.

2½ cups (20 fl oz/625 ml) water

1 cup (7 oz/220 g) jasmine rice

1 tablespoon unsalted butter

¼ teaspoon salt

1½ cups (12 fl oz/375 ml) coconut milk

⅓ cup (2 oz/90 g) firmly packed palm or brown sugar

1 tablespoon lime juice

1 teaspoon finely grated kaffir lime zest or regular lime zest

½ cup (4 oz/125 g) mango, peeled and sliced or diced

1 kaffir lime leaf, finely sliced, or thin strips of zest from 1 lime (optional)

Combine water, rice, butter and salt in pressure cooker. Lock lid in place and bring to high pressure over high heat. Reduce heat to a level that just maintains high pressure and cook for 8 minutes. Remove cooker from heat and quick-release pressure. Stir in coconut milk, scraping any rice from bottom of cooker. Stir in sugar, lime juice and zest. Simmer over medium heat, stirring constantly, until thickened, 4–6 minutes. Spoon into individual dishes and serve warm or chilled. Serve with mango or fold mango through rice. Garnish with lime leaves or lime zest, if desired.

Tip The addition of butter reduces possible foaming as rice cooks, which could clog the vent. Substitute butter with oil if preferred.

RHUBARB, PEARS AND APPLES WITH CINNAMON NUT TOPPING

SERVES 4–6

FOR TOPPING

1/3 cup (3 oz/90 g) unsalted butter

2/3 cup (2 oz/60 g) rolled oats

1/4 cup (1 1/2 oz/45 g) all-purpose (plain) flour

1/2 cup (3 1/2 oz/105 g) firmly packed brown sugar

1 teaspoon ground cinnamon

1/4 cup (1 oz/30 g) almonds, chopped

1 lb (500 g) rhubarb, cut into 3/4-inch (2-cm) pieces

2 pears such as Bartlett or Packham, about 1 lb (500 g) total, cut into 1-inch (2.5-cm) chunks

2 green apples such as Granny Smith, about 1 lb (500 g) total, cut into 1-inch (2.5-cm) chunks

1/2 cup (4 fl oz/125 ml) dry red wine such as Merlot

1/4 cup (2 oz/60 g) raw sugar or firmly packed brown sugar

1/2 teaspoon ground cinnamon

1 teaspoon lemon zest, finely grated

1 tablespoon glacé ginger, finely grated

vanilla ice cream

To make topping, melt butter in a small saucepan over medium-low heat. Add remaining ingredients and cook, stirring constantly, until mixture forms small clumps, about 5 minutes. Cover, remove from heat and keep warm.

Put rhubarb, pears, apples, wine, sugar, cinnamon and zest in pressure cooker. Lock lid in place and bring to high pressure over high heat. Immediately remove cooker from heat and allow pressure to reduce naturally for 10 minutes, then quick-release pressure. Stir in ginger. Divide fruit among individual dishes and spoon on topping. Accompany with scoops of ice cream.

GINGER-WALNUT CHEESECAKES

SERVES 4

FOR CRUST
5 or 6 ginger cookies, about 2 oz (60 g) total
⅓ cup (1 oz/30 g) finely crushed walnuts
2 tablespoons (1 oz/30g) unsalted butter, melted

FOR FILLING
1 lb (500 g) full-fat cream cheese, at room temperature
½ cup (8 oz/250 g) sugar
2 large eggs
1 tablespoon lime juice
2 teaspoons lime zest, finely grated

To make crust, put cookies in a plastic bag and finely crush using a meat mallet or rolling pin. In a bowl, stir together crushed cookies, walnuts and butter. Divide crust mixture among 4 lightly buttered 1-cup (8–fl oz/250-ml) ramekins or other molds, pressing it into place.

To make filling, put cream cheese and sugar in a food processor and process until smooth. Alternatively, put in a bowl and beat with an electric mixer. Add eggs, lime juice and lime zest and mix for 1 minute longer. Divide mixture evenly among ramekins. Cover top with aluminum foil, crimping edges to secure.

Pour 2 cups (16 fl oz/500 ml) water into pressure cooker. Place trivet in cooker. Arrange ramekins in steamer basket or on a plate that allows steam to circulate and place on trivet. Lock lid in place and bring to high pressure over high heat. Reduce heat to a level that just maintains high pressure and cook for 15 minutes. Remove cooker from heat and allow pressure to reduce naturally for 4 minutes, then quick-release pressure. Serve warm or cold. Alternatively, run a knife around edges of each ramekin and unmold cheesecake onto a plate.

Tip Serve the cheesecakes accompanied with fresh berries sweetened, if desired, with sugar. Fresh or frozen berries can be stirred into filling before dividing among ramekins.

INDEX

WEIGHTS AND MEASUREMENTS

The conversions given in the recipes in this book are approximate. Whichever system you use, remember to follow it consistently, to ensure that the proportions are consistent throughout a recipe.

Weights

Imperial	Metric
$1/3$ oz	10 g
$1/2$ oz	15 g
$3/4$ oz	20 g
1 oz	30 g
2 oz	60 g
3 oz	90 g
4 oz ($1/4$ lb)	125 g
5 oz ($1/3$ lb)	150 g
6 oz	180 g
7 oz	220 g
8 oz ($1/2$ lb)	250 g
9 oz	280 g
10 oz	300 g
11 oz	330 g
12 oz ($3/4$ lb)	375 g
16 oz (1 lb)	500 g
2 lb	1 kg
3 lb	1.5 kg
4 lb	2 kg

Volume

Imperial	Metric	Cup
1 fl oz	30 ml	
2 fl oz	60 ml	$1/4$
3 fl oz	90 ml	$1/3$
4 fl oz	125 ml	$1/2$
5 fl oz	150 ml	$2/3$
6 fl oz	180 ml	$3/4$
8 fl oz	250 ml	1
10 fl oz	300 ml	$1^1/4$
12 fl oz	375 ml	$1^1/2$
13 fl oz	400 ml	$1^2/3$
14 fl oz	440 ml	$1^3/4$
16 fl oz	500 ml	2
24 fl oz	750 ml	3
32 fl oz	1L	4

Oven temperature guide

The Celsius (°C) and Fahrenheit (°F) temperatures in this chart apply to most electric ovens. Decrease by 25°F or 10°C for a gas oven or refer to the manufacturer's temperature guide. For temperatures below 325°F (160°C), do not decrease the given temperature.

Oven description	°C	°F	Gas Mark
Cool	110	225	$1/4$
	130	250	$1/2$
Very slow	140	275	1
	150	300	2
Slow	170	325	3
Moderate	180	350	4
	190	375	5
Moderately hot	200	400	6
Fairly hot	220	425	7
Hot	230	450	8
Very hot	240	475	9
Extremely hot	250	500	10

Useful conversions

$1/4$ teaspoon	1.25 ml
$1/2$ teaspoon	2.5 ml
1 teaspoon	5 ml
1 Australian tablespoon	20 ml (4 teaspoons)
1 UK/US tablespoon	15 ml (3 teaspoons)

Butter/Shortening

1 tablespoon	$1/2$ oz	15 g
$1^1/2$ tablespoons	$3/4$ oz	20 g
2 tablespoons	1 oz	30 g
3 tablespoons	$1^1/2$ oz	45 g

A LANSDOWNE BOOK

Published by Apple Press in 2005
Sheridan House
4th Floor
112-116 Western Road
Hove
East Sussex BN3 1DD UK

www.apple-press.com

Created and produced by Lansdowne Publishing
Text: Brigid Treloar
Photographer: Andre Martin
Stylist: Sarah O'Brien
Designer: Avril Makula
Editor: Judith Dunham
Production: Sally Stokes and Eleanor Cant
Project Coordinator: Kate Merrifield

ISBN 1-84543-064-6

Set in Meta Plus and Bembo on QuarkXPress
Printed in Singapore by Tien Wah Press (Pte) Ltd